THE ROMAN RITUAL

HOLY COMMUNION AND WORSHIP OF THE
EUCHARIST OUTSIDE MASS

HOLY COMMUNION OUTSIDE MASS

Published by authority of the
Bishops' Committee on the Liturgy
National Conference of Catholic Bishops
Revised printing, June 28, 1983

Concordat cum Originali:
  + John S. Cummins, Bishop of Oakland
  Chairman, Bishops' Committee on the Liturgy
  National Conference of Catholic Bishops

Published by authority of the Bishops' Committee on the Liturgy, National Conference of Catholic Bishops. Revised printing, June 28, 1983.

© Copyright 1983
United States Catholic Conference
1312 Massachusetts Ave., N.W.
Washington, D.C. 20005
All rights reserved.

CONTENTS

FOREWORD

The Second Vatican Council repeatedly emphasized that the Eucharist is the center of Christian life and community. In the Decree on the Ministry of Life of Priests the Council Fathers wished to underscore this reality in the life of the Church when it said:

> No Christian community is ever built up unless it has its roots and center in the eucharistic liturgy, which, therefore, is the indispensable starting point for bringing people to a sense of community (*Presbyterorum Ordinis* 6).

Even when the Mass cannot be celebrated for the people the Church provides forms of participation in the eucharistic mystery by which they "are closely united with the sacrifice which perpetuates the sacrifice of the cross...(and become) sharers in the sacred banquet" (*Holy Communion outside Mass*, Introduction, 15).

The *Rite of Distributing Holy Communion outside Mass with the Celebration of the Word* may be used for those times when the Mass cannot be celebrated or in those instances when the faithful cannot legitimately be present at Mass. The rite is taken from the *Roman Ritual: Holy Communion and Worship of the Eucharist outside Mass* which was approved for use in the dioceses of the United States of America by the National Conference of Catholic Bishops in plenary assembly on 22 November 1974 and confirmed by the Apostolic See by decree of the Sacred Congregation for Divine Worship on 11 March 1975 (Prot. CD 408/75).

28 June 1983
Memorial of Saint Irenaeus,
   bishop and martyr

+ John S. Cummins, Bishop of Oakland
Chairman
Bishops' Conference on the Liturgy
National Conference of Catholic Bishops

SACRED CONGREGATION FOR DIVINE WORSHIP

Prot. no. 900/73

DECREE

The sacrament of the eucharist was entrusted by Christ to his bride, the Church, as spiritual nourishment and as a pledge of eternal life. The Church continues to receive this gift with faith and love.

The celebration of the eucharist in the sacrifice of the Mass is the true origin and purpose of the worship shown to the eucharist outside Mass. The principal reason for reserving the sacrament after Mass is to unite, through sacramental communion, the faithful unable to participate in the Mass, especially the sick and the aged, with Christ and the offering of his sacrifice.

In turn eucharistic reservation, which became customary in order to permit the reception of communion, led to the practice of adoring this sacrament and offering to it the worship which is due to God. This cult of adoration is based upon valid and solid principles. Moreover, some of the public and communal forms of this worship were instituted by the Church itself.

The rite of Mass has been revised and, in the instruction *Eucharisticum mysterium* of May 25, 1967, regulations have been published "on the practical arrangements for the cult of this sacrament even after Mass and its relationship to the proper ordering of the sacrifice of the Mass in the light of the regulations of the Second Vatican Council, and of other documents of the Apostolic See on this matter."[1] Now the Congregation for Divine Worship has revised the rites, "Holy Communion and the Worship of the Eucharist outside Mass."

These rites, approved by Pope Paul VI, are now published in this edition, which is declared to be the *editio typica*. They are to replace the rites which appear in the Roman Ritual at the present time. They may be used at once in Latin; they may be used in the vernacular from the day set by the episcopal conferences for their territory, after the conferences have prepared a vernacular version and have obtained the confirmation of the Apostolic See.

---

[1] See Congregation of Rites, instruction *Eucharisticum mysterium*, no. 3g: *AAS* 59 (1967) 543.

Anything to the contrary notwithstanding.

From the office of the Congregation for Divine Worship, June 21, 1973, the feast of Corpus Christi.

+ Arturo Cardinal Tabera
Prefect

+ Annibale Bugnini
Titular Archbishop of Diocletiana
Secretary

HOLY COMMUNION AND WORSHIP OF THE
EUCHARIST OUTSIDE OF MASS

GENERAL INTRODUCTION

I. The Relationship between Eucharistic Worship outside Mass and the Eucharistic Celebration

1. The celebration of the eucharist is the center of the entire Christian life, both for the Church universal and for the local congregations of the Church. "The other sacraments, all the ministries of the Church, and the works of the apostolate are united with the eucharist and are directed toward it. For the holy eucharist contains the entire spiritual treasure of the Church, that is, Christ himself, our passover and living bread. Through his flesh, made living and life-giving by the Holy Spirit, he offers life to men, who are thus invited and led to offer themselves, their work, and all creation together with him."[1]

2. "The celebration of the eucharist in the sacrifice of the Mass," moreover, "is truly the origin and the goal of the worship which is shown to the eucharist outside Mass."[2] Christ the Lord "is offered in the sacrifice of the Mass when he becomes present sacramentally as the spiritual food of the faithful under the appearance of bread and wine." And, "once the sacrifice is offered and while the eucharist is reserved in churches and oratories, he is truly Emmanuel, 'God with us.' He is in our midst day and night; full of grace and truth, he dwells among us."[3]

3. No one therefore may doubt "that all the faithful show this holy sacrament the veneration and adoration which is due to God himself, as has always been customary in the Catholic Church. Nor is the sacrament to be less the object of adoration because it was instituted by Christ the Lord to be received as food."[4]

4. In order to direct and to encourage devotion to the sacrament of the eucharist correctly, the eucharistic mystery must be considered in all its fullness, both in the celebration of Mass and in the worship of the sacrament which is reserved after Mass to extend the grace of the sacrifice.[5]

II. The Purpose of Eucharistic Reservation

5. The primary and original reason for reservation of the eucharist outside Mass is the administration of viaticum. The secondary reasons are the giving of communion and the adoration of our Lord Jesus Christ who is present in the sacrament. The reservation of the sacrament for the sick led to the praiseworthy practice of adoring this heavenly food in the churches. This cult of adoration rests upon an authentic and solid basis, especially because

faith in the real presence of the Lord leads naturally to external, public expression of that faith.[6]

6. In the celebration of Mass the chief ways in which Christ is present in his Church gradually become clear. First he is present in the very assembly of the faithful, gathered together in his name; next he is present in his word, when the Scriptures are read in the Church and explained; then in the person of the minister; finally and above all, in the eucharistic sacrament. In a way that is completely unique, the whole and entire Christ, God and man, is substantially and permanently present in the sacrament. This presence of Christ under the appearance of bread and wine "is called real, not to exclude other kinds of presence as if they were not real, but because it is real *par excellence.*"[7]

Therefore, to express the sign of the eucharist, it is more in harmony with the nature of the celebration that, at the altar where Mass is celebrated, there should if possible be no reservation of the sacrament in the tabernacle from the beginning of Mass. The eucharistic presence of Christ is the fruit of the consecration and should appear to be such.[8]

7. The consecrated hosts are to be frequently renewed and reserved in a ciborium or other vessel, in a number sufficient for the communion of the sick and others outside Mass.[9]

8. Pastors should see that churches and public oratories where, according to law, the holy eucharist is reserved, are open every day at least for some hours, at a convenient time, so that the faithful may easily pray in the presence of the blessed sacrament.[10]

III. The Place of Eucharistic Reservation

9. The place for the reservation of the eucharist should be truly preeminent. It is highly recommended that the place be suitable also for private adoration and prayer so that the faithful may easily, fruitfully, and constantly honor the Lord, present in the sacrament, through personal worship.

This will be achieved more easily if the chapel is separate from the body of the church, especially in churches where marriages and funerals are celebrated frequently and churches which are much visited by pilgrims or because of their artistic and historical treasures.

10. The holy eucharist is to be reserved in a solid tabernacle. It must be opaque and unbreakable. Ordinarily there should be only one tabernacle in a church; this may be placed on an altar or, at the discretion of the local Ordinary, in some other noble and properly ornamented part of the church other than an altar.[11]

The key to the tabernacle where the eucharist is reserved must be kept most carefully by the priest in charge of the church or oratory or by a special minister who has received the faculty to give communion.

11. The presence of the eucharist in the tabernalce is to be shown by a veil or in another suitable way determined by the competent authority.

According to traditional usage, an oil lamp or lamp with a wax candle is to burn constantly near the tabernacle as a sign of the honor which is shown to the Lord.[12]

IV. The Competence of Episcopal Conferences

12. It is for episcopal conferences, in the preparation of particular rituals in accord with the Constitution on the Liturgy (no. 63b), to accommodate this title of the Roman Ritual to the needs of individual regions so that, their actions having been confirmed by the Apostolic See, the ritual may be followed in the respective regions.

In this matter it will be for the conferences:

a) to consider carefully and prudently what elements, if any, of popular traditions may be retained or introduced, provided they can be harmonized with the spirit of the liturgy, and then to propose to the Apostolic See the adaptations they judge necessary or useful; these may be introduced with the consent of the Apostolic See;

b) to prepare translations of texts which are truly accommodated to the character of various languages and the mentality of various cultures; they may add texts, especially for singing, with appropriate melodies.

NOTES

[1] Second Vatican Council, decree *Prebyterorum ordinis.* no. 5.
[2] Congregation of Rites instruction *Eucharisticum mysterium*, no. 3e; *AAS* 59 (1967) 542.
[3] *Ibid.*, no. 36: *loc. cit.* 541; Paul VI, encyclical *Mysterium fidei*, near the end: *AAS* 57 (1965) 771.
[4] Congregation of Rites, instruction *Eucharisticum mysterium*, no. 3f: *AAS* 59 (1967) 543.
[5] See *ibid.*, no. 3g: *loc. cit.* 543.
[6] See *ibid.*, no. 49: *loc. cit.* 566–567.
[7] Paul VI, encyclical *Mysterium fidel: AAS* 57 (1965) 764; see Congregation of Rites, instruction *Eucharisticum mysterium*, no. 55: *AAS* 59 (1967) 568–569.
[8] See Congregation of Rites, instruction *Eucharisticum mysterium*, no. 55: *AAS* 59 (1967) 568–569.
[9] See Roman Missal, General Instruction, nos. 285 and 292.
[10] See Congregation of Rites, instruction *Eucharisticum mysterium*, no. 51: *AAS* 59 (1967) 567.
[11] See *ibid.*, nos. 52–53: *loc. cit.* 567–568.
[12] See *ibid.*, no. 57: *loc. cit.* 569.

INTRODUCTION TO
HOLY COMMUNION OUTSIDE MASS

I. The Relationship between Communion outside Mass and the Sacrifice

13. Sacramental communion received during Mass is the more perfect participation in the eucharistic celebration. The eucharistic sign is expressed more clearly when the faithful receive the body of the Lord from the same sacrifice after the communion of the priest.[1] Therefore, recently baked bread, for the communion of the faithful, should ordinarily be consecrated in every eucharistic celebration.

14. The faithful should be encouraged to receive communion during the eucharistic celebration itself.

Priests, however, are not to refuse to give communion to the faithful who ask for it even outside Mass.[2]

In fact it is proper that those who are prevented from being present at the community's celebration should be refreshed with the eucharist. In this way they may realize that they are united not only with the Lord's sacrifice but also with the community itself and are supported by the love of their brothers and sisters.

Pastors should see that an opportunity to receive the eucharist is given to the sick and aged, even though not gravely sick or in imminent danger of death, frequently and, if possible, daily, especially during the Easter season. It is lawful to minister communion under the appearance of wine to those who cannot receive the consecrated bread.[3]

15. The faithful should be instructed carefully that, even when they receive communion outside Mass, they are closely united with the sacrifice which perpetuates the sacrifice of the cross. They are sharers in the sacred banquet in which "by communion in the body and blood of the Lord the people of God shares in the blessings of the paschal sacrifice, renews the new covenant once made by God with men in the blood of Christ, and by faith and hope prefigures and anticipates the eschatological banquet in the kingdom of the Father, proclaiming the death of the Lord until he comes."[4]

II. The Time of Communion outside Mass

16. Communion may be given outside Mass on any day and at any hour. It is proper, however, to determine the hours for giving communion, with a view to the convenience of the faithful, so that the celebration may take place in a fuller form and with greater spiritual benefit.

Nevertheless:

a) on Holy Thursday, communion may be given only during Mass; communion may be brought to the sick at any hour of the day;

b) on Good Friday communion may be given only during the celebration of the Passion of the Lord; communion may be brought to the sick who cannot participate in the celebration at any hour of the day;

c) on Holy Saturday communion may be given only as viaticum.[5]

III. The Minister of Communion

17. It is, first of all, the office of the priest and the deacon to minister holy communion to the faithful who ask to receive it.[6] It is most fitting, therefore, that they give a suitable part of their time to this ministry of their order, depending on the needs of the faithful.

It is the office of an acolyte who has been properly instituted to give communion as a special minister when the priest and deacon are absent or impeded by sickness, old age, or pastoral ministry or when the number of the faithful at the holy table is so great that the Mass or other service may be unreasonably protracted.[7]

The local Ordinary may give other special ministers the faculty to give communion whenever it seems necessary for the pastoral benefit of the faithful and a priest, deacon, or acolyte is not available.[8]

IV. The Place of Communion outside Mass

18. The place where communion outside Mass is ordinarily given is a church or oratory in which the eucharist is regularly celebrated or reserved or a church, oratory, or other place where the local community regularly gathers for the liturgical assembly on Sundays or other days. Communion may be given, however, in other places, including private homes, when it is a question of the sick, prisoners, or others who cannot leave the place without danger or serious difficulty.

V. Regulations for Giving Communion

19. When communion is given in a church or oratory, a corporal is to be placed on the altar, which is already covered with a cloth.[9] A communion plate is to be used.

When communion is given in other places, a suitable table is to be prepared and covered with a cloth; candles are also to be provided.

20. The minister of communion, if he is a priest or deacon, is to be vested in an alb, or a surplice over a cassock, and a stole.

Other ministers should wear either the liturgical vesture which may be traditional in their region or the vestment which is appropriate for this ministry and has been approved by the Ordinary.

The eucharist for communion outside a church is to be carried in a pyx or other covered vessel; the vesture of the minister and the manner of carrying the eucharist should be appropriate and in accord with local circumstances.

21. In giving communion the custom of placing the particle of consecrated bread on the tongue of the communicant is to be maintained because it is based on a tradition of several centuries.

Episcopal conferences, however, may decree, their actions having been confirmed by the Apostolic See, that communion may also be given in their territories by placing the consecrated bread in the hands of the faithful, provided there is no danger of irreverence or false opinions about the eucharist entering the minds of the faithful.[10]

The faithful should be instructed that Jesus Christ is Lord and Savior and that, present in the sacrament, he must be given the same worship and adoration which is to be given to God.[11]

In either case, communion must be given by the competent minister, who shows the particle of consecrated bread to the communicant and gives it to him, saying *The body of Christ*, to which the communicant replies *Amen*.

In the case of communion under the appearance of wine, the regulations of the instruction *Sacramentali Communione* of June 29, 1970, are to be followed exactly.[12]

22. Fragments which may remain after communion are to be reverently gathered and placed in a ciborium or in a vessel with water.

Likewise, if communion is given under the appearance of wine, the chalice or other vessel is to be washed with water.

The water used for cleansing the vessels may be drunk or poured out in a suitable place.

VI. Dispositions for Communion

23. The eucharist continuously makes present among men the paschal mystery of Christ. It is the source of every grace and of the forgiveness of sins. Nevertheless, those who intend to receive the body of the Lord must

approach it with a pure conscience and proper dispositions of soul if they are to receive the effects of the paschal sacrament.

On this account the Church prescribes "that no one conscious of mortal sin, even though he seems to be contrite, may go to the holy eucharist without previous sacramental confession."[13] In urgent necessity and if no confessor is available, he should simply make an act of perfect contrition with the intention of confessing individually, at the proper time, the mortal sins which he cannot confess at present.

It is desirable that those, who receive communion daily or very often, go to the sacrament of penance at regular intervals, depending on their circumstances.

Besides this, the faithful should look upon the eucharist as an antidote which frees them from daily faults and keeps them from mortal sins; they should also understand the proper way to use the penitential parts of the liturgy, especially at Mass.[14]

24. Communicants are not to receive the sacrament unless they have fasted for one hour from solid food and beverages, with the exception of water.

The period of the eucharistic fast, that is, abstinence from food or alcoholic drink, is reduced to about a quarter of an hour for:

1) the sick who are living in hospitals or at home, even if they are not confined to bed;

2) the faithful of advanced age, even if not bedridden, whether they are confined to their homes because of old age or live in a nursing home;

3) sick priests, even if not bedridden, or elderly priests, whether they are to celebrate Mass or to receive communion;

4) persons who care for the sick or aged, and the family of the sick or aged, who wish to receive communion with them, when they cannot conveniently observe the fast of one hour.[15]

25. The union with Christ, to which the sacrament is directed, should be extended to the whole of Christian life. Thus the faithful, constantly reflecting upon the gift they have received, should carry on their daily work with thanksgiving, under the guidance of the Holy Spirit, and should bring forth fruits of rich charity.

So that they may continue more easily in the thanksgiving which is offered to God in an excellent manner through the Mass, it is recommended that each one who has been refreshed by communion should remain in prayer for a period of time.[16]

NOTES

[1] See Second Vatican Council, constitution *Sacrosanctum Concilium*, no. 55.

[2] See Congregation of Rites, instruction *Eucharisticum mysterium*, no. 33a: *AAS* 59 (1967) 559–560.

[3] See *ibid.*, nos. 40–41: *loc. cit.* 562–563.

[4] *Ibid.*, no. 3a: *loc. cit.*, 541–542.

[5] See Roman Missal, typical edition 1970; *Missa vespertina in Cena Domini*, 243; *Celebratio Passionis Domini*, 250, no. 3; *Sabbato sancto*, 265.

[6] See Congregation of Rites, instruction *Eucharisticum mysterium*, no. 31: *AAS* 59 (1967).

[7] See Paul VI, apostolic letter *Ministeria quaedam*, August 15, 1972, no. VI: *AAS* 64 (1972) 532.

[8] See Congregation for the Discipline of the Sacraments, instruction *Immensae caritatis*, January 29, 1973, no. 4.

[9] See Roman Missal, *General Instruction*, no. 269.

[10] See Congregation for Divine Worship, instruction *Memoriale Domini*, May 29, 1969: *AAS* 61 (1969) 541–555.

[11] See Congregation for the Discipline of the Sacraments, instruction *Immensae caritatis*, January 21, 1973, no. 4.

[12] See no. 6: *AAS* 62 (1970) 665–666.

[13] See Council of Trent, Session XIII, Decree on the Eucharist, 7: Denz.-Schön. 1646–1647; *ibid.*, Session XIV *Canones de sacramento Paenitentiae*; 9: Denz.-Schön. 1709; Congregation for the Doctrine of the Faith, *Normæ pastorales circa absolutionem sacramentalem generali modo impertiendam*, June 16, 1972, introduction and no. VI: *AAS* 64 (1972) 510 and 512.

[14] See Congregation of Rites, instruction *Eucharisticum mysterium*, no. 35: *AAS* 59 (1967) 561.

[15] See Congregation for the Discipline of the Sacraments, instruction *Immensae caritatis*, January 29, 1973, no. 3.

[16] See Congregation of Rites, instruction *Eucharisticum mysterium*, no. 38: *AAS* (1967) 562.

RITE OF DISTRIBUTING HOLY COMMUNION
OUTSIDE MASS
WITH THE CELEBRATION OF THE WORD

26. This rite is to be used chiefly when Mass is not celebrated or when communion is not distributed at scheduled times. The purpose is that the people should be nourished by the word of God. By hearing it they learn that the marvels it proclaims reach their climax in the paschal mystery of which the Mass is a sacramental memorial and in which they share by communion. Nourished by God's word, they are led on to grateful and fruitful participation in the saving mysteries.

INTRODUCTORY RITES

27. After the people have assembled and preparations for the service (see nos. 19–20) are complete, all stand for the greeting of the minister.

Greeting

If he is a priest or deacon, he says:

The grace of our Lord Jesus Christ and the love of God and the fellowship of the Holy Spirit be with you all.

The people answer:

And also with you.

Or:

The Lord be with you.

The people answer:

And also with you.

Or:

**The grace and peace of God our Father
and the Lord Jesus Christ be with you.**

The people answer:

Blessed be the God and Father of our Lord
Jesus Christ.

or:

And also with you.

Any other customary forms of greeting from scripture may be used.

If the minister is not a priest or deacon, he greets those present with
these or similar words:

**Brothers and sisters,
the Lord invites us (you) to his table
to share in the body of Christ:
bless him for his goodness.**

The people answer:

Blessed be God for ever.

Penitential Rite

28. The penitential rite follows, and the minister invites the people to
recall their sins and to repent of them in these words:

**My brothers and sisters,
to prepare ourselves for this celebration,
let us call to mind our sins.**

A pause for silent reflection follows.

All say:

> I confess to almighty God,
> and to you, my brothers and sisters,
> that I have sinned through my own fault

They strike their breast:

> in my thoughts and in my words,
> in what I have done,
> and in what I have failed to do;
> and I ask blessed Mary, ever virgin,
> all the angels and saints,
> and you, my brothers and sisters,
> to pray for me to the Lord our God.

The minister concludes:

> **May almighty God have mercy on us,**
> **forgive us our sins,**
> **and bring us to everlasting life.**

The people answer:

> Amen.

Or: [190]

The minister invites the people to recall their sins and to repent of them in these words:

> **My brothers and sisters,**
> **to prepare ourselves for this celebration,**
> **let us call to mind our sins.**

A pause for silent reflection follows.

The minister says:

Lord, we have sinned against you.

The people answer:

> Lord, have mercy.

Minister:

> **Lord, show us your mercy and love.**

The people answer:

> And grant us your salvation.

The minister concludes:

> **May almighty God have mercy on us,**
> **forgive us our sins,**
> **and bring us to everlasting life.**

The people answer:

> Amen.

Or: [191]

The minister invites the people to recall their sins and to repent of them in these words:

> **My brothers and sisters,**
> **to prepare ourselves for this celebration,**
> **let us call to mind our sins.**

A pause for silent reflection follows.

The minister, or someone else, makes the following or other invocations:

Minister:

> **You brought us to salvation by your paschal**
> **mystery:**
> **Lord, have mercy.**

The people answer:

Lord, have mercy.

Minister:

You renew us by the wonders of your passion:
Christ, have mercy.

The people answer:

Christ, have mercy.

Minister:

You give us your body to make us one
with your Easter sacrifice:
Lord, have mercy.

The people answer:

Lord, have mercy.

The minister concludes:

May almighty God have mercy on us,
forgive us our sins,
and bring us to everlasting life.

The people answer:

Amen.

CELEBRATION OF THE WORD OF GOD

29. The Liturgy of the Word now takes place as at Mass. Texts are chosen for the occasion either from the Mass of the day or from the votive Masses of the Holy Eucharist or the Precious Blood, the readings from which are in the Lectionary. A list of these passages can be found in the Appendix of this Ritual. The Lectionary offers a wide range of readings which may be drawn upon for particular needs, such as the votive Mass of the Sacred Heart.

There may be one or more readings, the first being followed by a psalm or some other chant or by a period of silent prayer.

The celebration of the word ends with the general intercessions.

THE SHORT FORM OF THE READING OF THE WORD *

[44]

Omitting the celebration of the word of God, the minister or other person should read a short scriptural text referring to the bread of life.

John 6:54-55

> He who feeds on my flesh
> and drinks my blood
> has life eternal,
> and I will raise him up on the last day.
> For my flesh is real food
> and my blood real drink.

John 6:54-58

> He who feeds on my flesh
> and drinks my blood
> has life eternal,
> and I will raise him up on the last day.
> For my flesh is real food
> and my blood is real drink.
> The man who feeds on my flesh
> and drinks my blood
> remains in me, and I in him.
> Just as the Father who has life sent me
> and I have life because of the Father,
> so the man who feeds on me
> will have life because of me.
> This is the bread that came down from heaven.
> Unlike your ancestors who ate and died
>   nonetheless,
> the man who feeds on this bread shall live forever.

---

*42. This form of service is used when the longer, more elaborate form is unsuitable, especially when there are only one or two for communion and a true community celebration is impossible.

John 14:6

> **Jesus told him:**
> **"I am the way, and the truth, and the life;**
> **no one comes to the Father but through me."**

John 14:23

> **Jesus answered:**
> **"Anyone who loves me**
> **will be true to my word,**
> **and my Father will love him;**
> **we will come to him**
> **and make our dwelling place with him."**

John 15:4

> **Live on in me, as I do in you.**
> **No more than a branch can bear fruit of itself**
> **apart from the vine,**
> **can you bear fruit**
> **apart from me.**

1 Corinthians 11:26

> **Every time, then, you eat this bread and**
> **drink this cup,**
> **You proclaim the death of the Lord until he**
> **comes.**

1 John 4:16

> **We have come to know and to believe**
> **in the love God has for us.**
> **God is love,**
> **and he who abides in love**
> **abides in God,**
> **and God in him.**

30. After the prayer the minister goes to the place where the sacrament is reserved, takes the ciborium or pyx containing the body of the Lord, places it on the altar and genuflects. He then introduces the Lord's Prayer in these or similar words:

> **Let us pray with confidence to the Father**
> **in the words our Savior gave us:**

He continues with the people:

> **Our Father . . .**

31. The minister may invite the people in these or similar words:

> **Let us offer each other the sign of peace.**

All make an appropriate sign of peace, according to local custom.

32. The minister genuflects. Taking the host, he raises it slightly over the vessel or pyx and, facing the people, says:

> **This is the Lamb of God**
> **who takes away the sins of the world.**
> **Happy are those who are called to his supper.**

The communicants say once:

> Lord, I am not worthy to receive you,
> but only say the word and I shall be healed.

33. If the minister receives communion, he says quietly:

> **May the body of Christ bring me to**
> **everlasting life.**

He reverently consumes the body of Christ.

34. Then he takes the vessel or pyx and goes to the communicants. He takes a host for each one, raises it slightly, and says:

The body of Christ.

The communicant answers:

Amen,

and receives communion.

35. During the distribution of communion, a hymn may be sung.

36. After communion the minister puts any particle left on the plate into the pyx, and he may wash his hands. He returns any remaining hosts to the tabernacle and genuflects.

37. A period of silence may now be observed, or a psalm or song of praise may be sung.

38. The minister then says the concluding prayer:

Let us pray.

**Lord Jesus Christ,
you gave us the eucharist
as the memorial of your suffering and death.
May our worship of this sacrament of your
    body and blood
help us to experience the salvation you won
    for us
and the peace of the kingdom
where you live with the Father and the
    Holy Spirit,
one God, for ever and ever.**

The people answer:

Amen.

Other prayers may be chosen: [210]

Father,
you have brought to fulfillment the work of
**   our redemption**
through the Easter mystery of Christ your Son.
May we who faithfully proclaim his death and
**   resurrection in these sacramental signs**
experience the constant growth of your
**   salvation in our lives.**

We ask this through Christ our Lord.

Or: [211]

Lord,
you have nourished us with one bread from
**   heaven.**
Fill us with your Spirit,
and make us one in peace and love.

We ask this through Christ our Lord.

Or: [212]

Lord,
may our sharing at this holy table make us holy.
By the body and blood of Christ
join all your people in brotherly love.

We ask this through Christ our Lord.

Or: [213]

Father,
you give us food from heaven.
By our sharing in this mystery
teach us to judge wisely the things of earth
and to love the things of heaven.

Grant this through Christ our Lord.

Or: [214]

Lord,
we give thanks for these holy mysteries
which bring to us here on earth
a share in the life to come,
through Christ our Lord.

Or: [215]

All-powerful God,
you renew us with your sacraments.
Help us to thank you by lives of faithful service.

We ask this through Christ our Lord.

Or: [216]

God our Father,
you give us a share in the one bread and the
    one cup
and make us one in Christ.
Help us to bring your salvation and joy
to all the world.

We ask this through Christ our Lord.

Or: [217]

Lord,
you renew us at your table with the bread of life.
May this food strengthen us in love
and help us to serve you in each other.

We ask this in the name of Jesus the Lord.

Or: [218]

Lord,
we thank you for the nourishment you give us
through your holy gift.

Pour out your Spirit upon us
and in the strength of this food from heaven
keep us single-minded in your service.

We ask this in the name of Jesus the Lord.

Or: [219]

Lord,
we are renewed by the breaking of one bread.
Keep us in your love
and help us to live the new life Christ won for us.

Grant this in the name of Jesus the Lord.

During the Easter season the following prayers are preferred:

[220]

Lord,
you have nourished us with your Easter
    sacraments.
Fill us with your Spirit
and make us one in peace and love.

We ask this through Christ our Lord.

Or: [221]

Lord,
may this sharing in the sacrament of your Son
free us from our old life of sin
and make us your new creation.

We ask this in the name of Jesus the Lord.

Or: [222]

Almighty and ever-living Lord,
you restored us to life
by raising Christ from death.

**Strengthen us by this Easter sacrament;
may we feel its saving power in our daily life.**

We ask this through Christ our Lord.

CONCLUDING RITE

39. If the minister is a priest or deacon, he extends his hands and, facing the people, says:

The Lord be with you.

The people answer:

And also with you.

He blesses the people with these words:

**May almighty God bless you,
the Father, and the Son, ✚ and the Holy
Spirit.**

The people answer:

Amen.

Instead of this formula a solemn blessing or prayer over the people may be used, as in the concluding rite of Mass in the Roman Missal (see Appendix II).

40. If the minister is not a priest or a deacon, he invokes God's blessing and, crossing himself, says:

**May the Lord bless us,
protect us from all evil
and bring us to everlasting life.**

or:

**May the almighty and merciful God bless and
protect us, the Father, and the Son, ✚ and the
Holy Spirit.**

The people answer:

Amen.

⎣_____⎦

41. Finally the minister says:

Go in the peace of Christ.

The people answer:

Thanks be to God.

Then after the customary reverence, the minister leaves.

APPENDIX I*

BIBLICAL READINGS

READINGS FROM THE OLD TESTAMENT

[113.]   Genesis 14:18-20

A reading from the book of Genesis

Melchizedek offered bread and wine to God.

Melchizedek, king of Salem, brought out bread and wine, and being a priest of God Most High, he blessed Abram with these words:

"Blessed be Abram by God Most High,
    the creator of heaven and earth;
And blessed be God Most High,
    who delivered your foes into your hand."

Then Abram gave him a tenth of everything.

[114.]   Exodus 12:21-27

A reading from the book of Exodus

When the Lord sees the blood on the door,
he will pass over your home.

Moses called all the elders of Israel and said to them, "Go and procure lambs for your families, and slaughter them as Passover victims. Then take a bunch of hyssop, and dipping it in the blood that is in the basin, sprinkle the lintel and the two doorposts with this blood. But none of you shall go outdoors until morning. For the Lord will go by, striking down the Egyptians. Seeing the blood on the lintel and the two doorposts, the Lord will pass over that door and not let the destroyer come into your houses to strike you down.

---

*For the sake of completeness we have provided excerpts from the Lectionary.

"You shall observe this as a perpetual ordinance for yourselves and your descendants. Thus, you must also observe this rite when you have entered the land which the Lord will give you as he promised. When your children ask you, 'What does this rite of yours mean?' you shall reply, 'This is the Passover sacrifice of the Lord, who passed over the houses of the Israelites in Egypt; when he struck down the Egyptians, he spared our houses'."

[115.]   Exodus 16:2-4, 12-15

A reading from the book of Exodus
The Lord will rain bread on us from heaven.

In the desert the whole Israelite community grumbled against Moses and Aaron. The Israelites said to them, "Would that we had died at the Lord's hand in the land of Egypt, as we sat by our fleshpots and ate our fill of bread! But you had to lead us into this desert to make the whole community die of famine!"

Then the Lord said to Moses, "I will now rain down bread from heaven for you. Each day the people are to go out and gather their daily portion; thus will I test them, to see whether they follow my instructions or not. I have heard the grumbling of the Israelites. Tell them: In the evening twilight you shall eat flesh, and in the morning you shall have your fill of bread, so that you may know that I, the Lord, am your God."

In the evening quail came up and covered the camp. In the morning a dew lay all about the camp, and when the dew evaporated, there on the surface of the desert were fine flakes like hoarfrost on the ground. On seeing it, the Israelites asked one another, "What is this?" for they did not know what it was. But Moses told them, "This is the bread which the Lord has given you to eat."

A reading from the book of Exodus

This is the blood marking the covenant the
Lord has made with you.

When Moses came to the people and related all the words and
ordinances of the Lord, they all answered with one voice, "We
will do everything that the Lord has told us." Moses then wrote
down all the words of the Lord and, rising early the next day, he
erected at the foot of the mountain an altar and twelve pillars
for the twelve tribes of Israel. Then, having sent certain young
men of the Israelites to offer holocausts and sacrifice young
bulls as peace offerings to the Lord, Moses took half of the blood
and put it in large bowls; the other half he splashed on the altar.
Taking the book of the covenant, he read it aloud to the people,
who answered, "All that the Lord has said, we will heed and
do." Then he took the blood and sprinkled it on the people, saying, "This is the blood of the covenant which the Lord has made
with you in accordance with all these words of his."

A reading from the book of Deuteronomy

He gave you food finer than any you have ever known.

Moses said to the people: "Remember how for forty years
now the Lord, your God, has directed all your journeying in the
desert, so as to test you by affliction and find out whether or not
it was your intention to keep his commandments. He therefore
let you be afflicted with hunger, and then fed you with manna, a
food unknown to you and your fathers, in order to show you
that not by bread alone does man live, but by every word that
comes forth from the mouth of the Lord.

"Remember the Lord, your God, who brought you out of the land of Egypt, that place of slavery; who guided you through the vast and terrible desert with its saraph serpents and scorpions, its parched and waterless ground; who brought forth water for you from the flinty rock and fed you in the desert with manna, a food unknown to your fathers."

[118.]   1 Kings 19:4-8

A reading from the first book of Kings

In the strength of that food, Elijah walked to the
mountain of God.

Elijah left his servant at Beersheba of Judah and went a day's journey into the desert, until he came to a broom tree and sat beneath it. He prayed for death: "This is enough, O Lord! Take my life, for I am no better than my fathers." He lay down and fell asleep under the broom tree, but then an angel touched him and ordered him to get up and eat. He looked and there at his head was a hearth cake and a jug of water. After he ate and drank, he lay down again, but the angel of the Lord came back a second time, touched him, and ordered, "Get up and eat, else the journey will be too long for you!" He got up, ate and drank; then, strengthened by that food, he walked forty days and forty nights to the mountain of God, Horeb.

A reading from the book of Proverbs

Eat the bread and drink the wine which I
have prepared for you.

Wisdom has built her house,
she has set up her seven columns;
She has dressed her meat, mixed her wine,
yes, she has spread her table.
She has sent out her maidens; she calls
from the heights out over the city:
"Let whoever is simple turn in here;
to him who lacks understanding, I say,
Come, eat of my food,
and drink of the wine I have mixed!
Forsake foolishness that you may live;
advance in the way of understanding."

READINGS FROM THE NEW TESTAMENT

[120.]   Acts 2:42-47

A reading from the Acts of the Apostles

They continued in fellowship with the apostles
and in the breaking of bread.

The brethren devoted themselves to the apostles' instruction
and the communal life, to the breaking of bread and the prayers. A reverent fear overtook them all, for many wonders and
signs were performed by the apostles. Those who believed
shared all things in common; they would sell their property and
goods, dividing everything on the basis of each one's need. They
went to the temple area together every day, while in their
homes they broke bread. With exultant and sincere hearts they
took their meals in common, praising God and winning the ap-
proval of all the people. Day by day the Lord added to their
number those who were being saved.

[121.]   Acts 10:34a, 37-43

A reading from the Acts of the Apostles

After he was raised from the dead, we ate and drank
with him.

Peter proceeded to address the people in these words: "I take
it you know what has been reported all over Judea about Jesus
of Nazareth, beginning in Galilee with the baptism John
preached; of the way God anointed him with the Holy Spirit and
power. He went about doing good works and healing all who
were in the grip of the devil, and God was with him. We are
witnesses to all that he did in the land of the Jews and in
Jerusalem. They killed him finally, 'hanging him on a tree,' only
to have God raise him up on the third day and grant that he be
seen, not by all, but only by such witnesses as had been chosen

beforehand by God—by us who ate and drank with him after he rose from the dead. He commissioned us to preach to the people and to bear witness that he is the one set apart by God as judge of the living and the dead. To him all the prophets testify, saying that everyone who believes in him has forgiveness of sins through his name."

[122.]   1 Corinthians 10:16-17

A reading from the first letter of Paul
to the Corinthians

Though we are many, we are one bread and one body.

Is not the cup of blessing we bless a sharing in the blood of Christ? And is not the bread we break a sharing in the body of Christ? Because the loaf of bread is one, we, many though we are, are one body, for we all partake of the one loaf.

[123.]   1 Corinthians 11:23-26

A reading from the first letter of Paul
to the Corinthians

Each time you eat this bread and drink this cup, you are proclaiming the death of the Lord Jesus.

I received from the Lord what I handed on to you, namely, that the Lord Jesus on the night in which he was betrayed took bread, and after he had given thanks, broke it and said, "This is my body, which is for you. Do this in remembrance of me." In the same way, after the supper, he took the cup, saying, "This cup is the new covenant in my blood. Do this, whenever you drink it, in remembrance of me." Every time, then, you eat this bread and drink this cup, you proclaim the death of the Lord until he comes!

A reading from the letter to the Hebrews

The blood of Christ purifies our hearts
from sin.

When Christ came as high priest of the good things which came to be, he entered once for all into the sanctuary, passing through the greater and more perfect tabernacle not made by hands, that is, not belonging to this creation. He entered, not with the blood of goats and calves but with his own blood, and achieved eternal redemption. For if the blood of goats and bulls and the sprinkling of a heifer's ashes can sanctify those who are defiled so that their flesh is cleansed, how much more will the blood of Christ, who through the eternal spirit offered himself up unblemished to God, cleanse our consciences from dead works to worship the living God!

This is why he is mediator of a new covenant: since his death has taken place for deliverance from transgressions committed under the first covenant, those who are called may receive the promised eternal inheritance.

[125.]   Hebrews 12:18-19, 22-24

A reading from the letter to the Hebrews

You have come to Mount Zion and to the city
of the living God.

You have not drawn near to an untouchable mountain and a blazing fire, and gloomy darkness and storm and trumpet blast, and a voice speaking words such that those who heard begged that they be not addressed to them. No, you have drawn near to Mount Zion and the city of the living God, the heavenly Jerusalem, to myriads of angels in festal gathering, to the assembly of the first-born enrolled in heaven, to God the judge of all, to the spirits of just men made perfect, to Jesus, the mediator of a new covenant.

A reading from the first letter of Peter

The ransom that was paid to free you was the
blood of the Lamb, Jesus Christ.

In prayer you call upon a Father who judges each one justly,
on the basis of his actions. Since this is so, conduct yourselves
reverently during your sojourn in a strange land. Realize that
you were delivered from the futile way of life your fathers
handed on to you, not by any diminishable sum of silver or gold
but by Christ's blood beyond all price: the blood of a spotless,
unblemished lamb chosen before the world's foundation and
revealed for your sake in these last days. It is through him that
you are believers in God, the God who raised him from the dead
and gave him glory. Your faith and hope, then, are centered in
God.

A reading from the first letter of John

There are three witnesses: the Spirit and
the water and the blood.

The love of God consists in this:
    that we keep his commandments—
    and his commandments are not burdensome.
Everyone begotten of God conquers the world
    and the power that has conquered the world
    is this faith of ours.
Who, then, is conqueror of the world?
    The one who believes that Jesus is the Son
    of God.

Jesus Christ it is who came through water and
    blood—
    not in water only,
    but in water and in blood.
It is the Spirit who testifies to this,
    and the Spirit is truth.
Thus there are three that testify,
    the Spirit and the water and the blood—
    and these three are of one accord.

[128.]   Revelation 1:5-8

A reading from the book of Revelation

Because he loves us, he has washed away our sins
with his blood.

[Grace and peace] from Jesus Christ the faithful witness, the
first-born from the dead and ruler of the kings of earth. To him
who loves us and freed us from our sins by his own blood, who
has made us a royal nation of priests in the service of his God
and Father—to him be glory and power forever and ever! Amen.

    See, he comes amid the clouds!
    Every eye shall see him,
    even of those who pierced him.
    All the peoples of the earth
    shall lament him bitterly.
    So it is to be! Amen!

    The Lord God says, "I am the Alpha and the Omega, the One
who is and was and who is to come, the Almighty!"

A reading from the book of Revelation

I saw an immense crowd, beyond hope of counting, of people from every nation, race, tribe and language.

I, John, saw before me a huge crowd which no one could count from every nation, race, people, and tongue. They stood before the throne and the Lamb, dressed in long white robes and holding palm branches in their hands. They cried out in a loud voice, "Salvation is from our God, who is seated on the throne, and from the Lamb!" All the angels who were standing around the throne and the elders and the four living creatures fell down before the throne to worship God. They said: "Amen! Praise and glory, wisdom, thanksgiving, and honor, power and might to our God forever and ever. Amen!"

Then one of the elders asked me, "Who do you think these are, all dressed in white? And where have they come from?" I said to him, "Sir, you should know better than I." He then told me, "These are the ones who have survived the great period of trial; they have washed their robes and made them white in the blood of the Lamb."

RESPONSORIAL PSALM

[130.]   Psalm 23:1-3, 4, 5, 6

Responsorial Psalm

℟. (1)   The Lord is my shepherd;
          there is nothing I shall want.

The Lord is my shepherd; I shall not want.
   In verdant pastures he gives me repose;
Beside restful waters he leads me;
   he refreshes my soul.

℟.   The Lord is my shepherd;
          there is nothing I shall want.

He guides me in right paths
   for his name's sake.
Even though I walk in the dark valley
   I fear no evil; for you are at my side
With your rod and your staff
   that give me courage.

℟.   The Lord is my shepherd;
          there is nothing I shall want.

You spread the table before me
   in the sight of my foes;
You anoint my head with oil;
   my cup overflows.

℟.   The Lord is my shepherd;
          there is nothing I shall want.

44

Only goodness and kindness follow me
    all the days of my life;
And I shall dwell in the house of the Lord
    for years to come.

R̸.   The Lord is my shepherd;
    there is nothing I shall want.

[131.]   Psalm 34: 2-3, 4-5, 6-7, 8-9

R̸. (9) Taste and see the goodness of the Lord.

I will bless the Lord at all times;
    his praise shall be ever in my mouth.
Let my soul glory in the Lord;
    the lowly will hear me and be glad.

R̸.   Taste and see the goodness of the Lord.

Glorify the Lord with me,
    let us together extol his name.
I sought the Lord, and he answered me
    and delivered me from all my fears.

R̸.   Taste and see the goodness of the Lord.

Look to him that you may be radiant with joy,
    and your faces may not blush with shame.
When the afflicted man called out, the
    Lord heard,
    and from all his distress he saved him.

R̸.   Taste and see the goodness of the Lord.

The angel of the Lord encamps
around those who fear him, and delivers
them.
Taste and see how good the Lord is;
happy the man who takes refuge in him.

℟. Taste and see the goodness of the Lord.

[132.]   Psalm 40:2, 4ab, 7-8a, 8b-9, 10

℟. (8.9) Here am I, Lord;
I come to do your will.

I have waited, waited for the Lord,
and he stooped toward me and heard my cry.
And he put a new song into my mouth,
a hymn to our God.

℟. Here am I, Lord;
I come to do your will.

Sacrifice or oblation you wished not,
but ears open to obedience you gave me.
Holocausts or sin-offerings you sought not;
then said I, "Behold, I come."

℟. Here am I, Lord;
I come to do your will.

"In the written scroll it is prescribed for me,
To do your will, O my God, is my delight,
and your law is within my heart!"

℟. Here am I, Lord;
I come to do your will.

I announced your justice in the vast
    assembly;
I did not restrain my lips, as you,
    O Lord, know.

℟.   Here am I, Lord;
    I come to do your will.

[133.]   Psalm 78:3-4a, 7ab, 23-24, 25 and 54

℟. (24) The Lord gave them bread from heaven.

What we have heard and know,
    and what our fathers have declared to us,
The glorious deeds of the Lord and his strength
    and the wonders that he wrought.

℟.   The Lord gave them bread from heaven.

He commanded the skies above
    and the doors of heaven he opened;
He rained manna upon them for food
    and gave them heavenly bread.

℟.   The Lord gave them bread from heaven.

The bread of the mighty was eaten by men;
    even a surfeit of provisions he sent them.
And he brought them to his holy land,
    to the mountains his right hand had won.

℟.   The Lord gave them bread from heaven.

R̷.   You are a priest for ever,
          in the line of Melchisedech.

**The Lord said to my Lord: "Sit at my right hand
    till I make your enemies your footstool."**

R̷.   You are a priest for ever,
          in the line of Melchisedech.

**The scepter of your power the Lord will
        stretch forth from Zion:
    "Rule in the midst of your enemies."**

R̷.   You are a priest for ever,
          in the line of Melchisedech.

**"Yours is princely power in the day of your
        birth, in holy splendor;
    before the daystar, like the dew, I have
        begotten you."**

R̷.   You are a priest for ever,
          in the line of Melchisedech.

R̷. (13) I will take the cup of salvation, and call on the
          name of the Lord.

**How shall I make a return to the Lord
    for all the good he has done for me?
The cup of salvation I will take up,
    and I will call upon the name of the Lord.**

℟.   I will take the cup of salvation, and call on the
name of the Lord.

Precious in the eyes of the Lord
  is the death of his faithful ones.
I am your servant, the son of your handmaid;
  you have loosed my bonds.

℟.   I will take the cup of salvation, and call on the
name of the Lord.

To you will I offer sacrifice of thanksgiving,
  and I will call upon the name of the Lord.
My vows to the Lord I will pay
  in the presence of all his people.

℟.   I will take the cup of salvation, and call on the
name of the Lord.

Or: (1 Cor 10: 16)

Our blessing-cup is a communion with the
blood of Christ.

[136.]   Psalm 145:10-11, 15-16, 17-18

℟. (16)   The hand of the Lord feeds us;
he answers all our needs.

Let all your works give you thanks, O Lord,
  and let your faithful ones bless you.
Let them discourse of the glory of your kingdom
  and speak of your might.

℟.   The hand of the Lord feeds us;
he answers all our needs.

The eyes of all look hopefully to you,
   and you give them their food in due season;
You open your hand
   and satisfy the desire of every living thing.

℟.   The hand of the Lord feeds us;
   he answers all our needs.

The Lord is just in all his ways
   and holy in all his works.
The Lord is near to all who call upon him,
   to all who call upon him in truth.

℟.   The hand of the Lord feeds us;
   he answers all our needs.

[137.]   Psalm 147:12-13, 14-15, 19-20

℟. (12a) Praise the Lord, Jerusalem.

Glorify the Lord, O Jerusalem;
   praise your God, O Zion.
For he has strengthened the bars of your gates,
   he has blessed your children within you.

℟.   Praise the Lord, Jerusalem.

He has granted peace in your borders;
   with the best of wheat he fills you.
He sends forth his command to the earth;
   swiftly runs his word!

℟.   Praise the Lord, Jerusalem.

He has proclaimed his word to Jacob,
  his statutes and his ordinances to Israel.
He has not done thus for any other nation;
  his ordinances he has not made known to
  them. Alleluia.

℟.   Praise the Lord, Jerusalem.

Or: (John 6:58c)
Whoever eats this bread will live for ever.

ALLELUIA VERSE
AND VERSE BEFORE THE GOSPEL

[138.]   John 6:51

I am the living bread from heaven, says the
    Lord;
if anyone eats this bread he will live for ever.

[139.]   John 6:56

Whoever eats my flesh and drinks my blood
will live in me and I in him, says the Lord.

[140.]   John 6:57

As the living Father sent me, and I live because
    of the Father,
so he who eats me will live because of me.

[141.]   Cf. Revelation 1:5ab

Jesus Christ, you are the faithful witness, first-
    born from the dead;
you have loved us and washed away our sins
    in your blood.

[142.]   Revelation 5:9

You are worthy O Lord, to receive the book
    and open its seals,
for you were killed, and have redeemed us for
    God in your blood.

GOSPEL

[143.]   Mark 14:12-16, 22-26

A reading from the holy gospel according to Mark

This is my body. This is my blood.

On the first day of Unleavened Bread, when it was customary to sacrifice the paschal lamb, his disciples said to Jesus, "Where do you wish us to go to prepare the Passover supper for you?" He sent two of his disciples with these instructions: "Go into the city and you will come upon a man carrying a water jar. Follow him. Whatever house he enters, say to the owner, 'The Teacher asks, Where is my guest room where I may eat the Passover with my disciples?' Then he will show you an upstairs room, spacious, furnished, and all in order. That is the place you are to get ready for us." The disciples went off. When they reached the city they found it just as he had told them, and they prepared the Passover supper.

During the meal he took bread, blessed and broke it, and gave it to them. "Take this," he said, "this is my body."

He likewise took a cup, gave thanks and passed it to them, and they all drank from it. He said to them: "This is my blood, the blood of the covenant, to be poured out on behalf of many. I solemnly assure you, I will never again drink the fruit of the vine until the day when I drink it new in the reign of God."

After singing songs of praise, they walked out to the Mount of Olives.

A reading from the holy gospel according to Mark

They dressed him up in purple and put a
crown of thorns on him.

The soldiers led Jesus away into the hall known as the praetorium; at the same time they assembled the whole cohort. They dressed him in royal purple, then wove a crown of thorns and put it on him, and began to salute him, "All hail! King of the Jews!" Continually striking Jesus on the head with a reed and spitting at him, they genuflected before him and pretended to pay him homage. When they had finished mocking him, they stripped him of the purple, dressed him in his own clothes, and led him out to crucify him.

[145.]   Luke 9:11b-17

A reading from the holy gospel according to Luke

All the people ate and were satisfied.

Jesus spoke to the crowd of the reign of God, and he healed all who were in need of healing.

As sunset approached the Twelve came and said to him, "Dismiss the crowd so that they can go into the villages and farms in the neighborhood and find themselves lodging and food, for this is certainly an out-of-the-way place." He answered them, "Why do you not give them something to eat yourselves?" They replied, "We have nothing but five loaves and two fishes. Or shall we ourselves go and buy food for all these people?" (There were about five thousand men.) Jesus said to his disciples, "Have them sit down in groups of fifty or so." They followed his instructions and got them all seated. Then, taking the five loaves and the two fishes, Jesus raised his eyes to heaven, pronounced a blessing over them, broke them, and gave them to his disciples for distribution to the crowd. They all ate until they had enough. What they had left, over and above, filled twelve baskets.

[146.]   Luke 22:39-44

A reading from the holy gospel according to Luke

While he prayed in agony, his sweat became
like drops of blood.

Jesus went out and made his way, as was his custom, to the Mount of Olives; his disciples accompanied him. On reaching the place he said to them, "Pray that you may not be put to the test." He withdrew from them about a stone's throw, then went down on his knees and prayed in these words: "Father, if it is your will, take this cup from me; yet not my will but yours be done." An angel then appeared to him from heaven to strengthen him. In his anguish he prayed with all the greater intensity, and his sweat became like drops of blood falling to the ground.

A reading from the holy gospel according to Luke

They recognized the Lord when he broke the
bread with them.

Two of the disciples of Jesus that same day [the first of the week] were making their way to a village named Emmaus seven miles distant from Jerusalem, discussing as they went all that had happened. In the course of their lively exchange, Jesus approached and began to walk along with them. However they were restrained from recognizing him. (He said to them, "What are you discussing as you go your way?" They halted in distress and one of them, Cleopas by name, asked him, "Are you the only resident of Jerusalem who does not know the things that went on there these past few days?" He said to them, "What things?" They said: "All those that had to do with Jesus of Nazareth, a prophet powerful in word and deed in the eyes of God and all the people; how our chief priests and leaders delivered him up to be condemned to death, and crucified him. We were hoping that he was the one who would set Israel free. Besides all this, today, the third day since these things happened, some women of our group have just brought us some astonishing news. They were at the tomb before dawn and failed to find his body, but returned with the tale that they had seen a vision of angels who declared he was alive. Some of our number went to the tomb and found it to be just as the women said; but him they did not see."

Then he said to them, "What little sense you have! How slow you are to believe all that the prophets have announced! Did not the Messiah have to undergo all this so as to enter into his glory?" Beginning, then, with Moses and all the prophets, he interpreted for them every passage of Scripture which referred to him.) By now they were near the village to which they were going, and he acted as if he were going farther. But they pressed him: "Stay with us. It is nearly evening—the day is practically over." So he went in to stay with them.

When he had seated himself with them to eat, he took bread, pronounced the blessing, then broke the bread and began to distribute it to them. With that their eyes were opened and they recognized him; whereupon he vanished from their sight. They said to one another, "Were not our hearts burning inside us as he talked to us on the road and explained the Scriptures to us?" They got up immediately and returned to Jerusalem, where they found the Eleven and the rest of the company assembled. They were greeted with "The Lord has been raised! It is true! He has appeared to Simon." Then they recounted what had happened on the road and how they had come to know him in the breaking of bread.

[148.]   John 6:1-15

A reading from the holy gospel according to John

He gave the people all the food they wanted.

Jesus crossed the Sea of Galilee [to the shore] of Tiberias; a vast crowd kept following him because they saw the signs he was performing for the sick. Jesus then went up the mountain and sat down there with his disciples. The Jewish feast of Passover was near; when Jesus looked up and caught sight of a vast crowd coming toward him, he said to Philip, "Where shall we buy bread for these people to eat?" (He knew well what he intended to do but he asked this to test Philip's response.) Philip replied, "Not even with two hundred days' wages could we buy loaves enough to give each of them a mouthful!"

One of Jesus's disciples, Andrew, Simon Peter's brother, remarked to him, "There is a lad here who has five barley loaves and a couple of dried fish, but what good is that for so many?" Jesus said, "Get the people to recline." Even though the men numbered about five thousand, there was plenty of grass for them to find a place on the ground. Jesus then took the loaves of bread, gave thanks, and passed them around to those reclining there; he did the same with the dried fish, as much as they wanted. When they had had enough, he told his disciples, "Gather up the crusts that are left over so that nothing will go to waste." At this, they gathered twelve baskets full of pieces left over by those who had been fed with the five barley loaves.

When the people saw the sign he had performed they began to say, "This is undoubtedly the Prophet who is to come into the world." At that, Jesus realized that they would come and carry him off to make him king, so he fled back to the mountain alone.

[149.]   John 6:24-35

A reading from the holy gospel according to John

If you come to me, you will never be hungry.
He who believes in me will never know thirst.

Once the crowd saw that neither Jesus nor his disciples were there, they too embarked in the boats and went to Capernaum looking for Jesus.

When they found him on the other side of the lake, they said to him, "Rabbi, when did you come here?" Jesus answered them:

"I assure you,
you are not looking for me because you have
   seen signs
but because you have eaten your fill of the
   loaves.
You should not be working for perishable food
but for food that remains unto life eternal,
food which the Son of Man will give you;
it is on him that God the Father has set
   his seal."

At this they said to him, "What must we do to perform the works of God?" Jesus replied:

"This is the work of God:
have faith in the One whom he sent."

"So that we can put faith in you," they asked him, "what sign are you going to perform for us to see? What is the 'work' you do? Our ancestors had manna to eat in the desert; according to Scripture, 'He gave them bread from the heavens to eat'." Jesus said to them:

"I solemnly assure you,
it was not Moses who gave you bread from
   the heavens;
it is my Father who gives you the real heavenly
   bread.
God's bread comes down from heaven
and gives life to the world."

"Sir, give us this bread always," they besought him.

Jesus explained to them:
"I myself am the bread of life.
No one who comes to me shall ever be hungry,
no one who believes in me shall thirst again."

A reading from the holy gospel according to John

I am the living bread from heaven.

At this the Jews started to murmur in protest against Jesus because he claimed, "I am the bread that came down from heaven." They kept saying: "Is this not Jesus, the son of Joseph? Do we not know his father and mother? How can he claim to have come down from heaven?"

"Stop your murmuring," Jesus told them.
"No one can come to me
unless the Father who sent me draws him;
I will raise him up on the last day.
It is written in the prophets:
'They shall all be taught by God.'
Everyone who has heard the Father
and learned from him
comes to me.
Not that anyone has seen the Father—
only the one who is from God
has seen the Father.
Let me firmly assure you,
he who believes has eternal life.
I am the bread of life.
Your ancestors ate manna in the desert, but
    they died.
This is the bread that comes down from heaven,
for a man to eat and never die.

"I myself am the living bread
come down from heaven.
If anyone eats this bread
he shall live forever."

A reading from the holy gospel according to John

My flesh and blood are true food and drink.

Jesus said to the crowd of the Jews:

"I myself am the living bread
come down from heaven.
If anyone eats this bread
he shall live forever;
the bread I will give
is my flesh for the life of the world."

At this the Jews quarreled among themselves, saying, "How
can he give us his flesh to eat?" Thereupon Jesus said to them:

"Let me solemnly assure you,
if you do not eat the flesh of the Son of Man
and drink his blood,
you have no life in you.
He who feeds on my flesh
and drinks my blood
has life eternal,
and I will raise him up on the last day.
For my flesh is real food
and my blood real drink.
The man who feeds on my flesh
and drinks my blood
remains in me, and I in him.
Just as the Father who has life sent me
and I have life because of the Father,
so the man who feeds on me
will have life because of me.
This is the bread that came down from heaven.
Unlike your ancestors who ate and died
    nonetheless,
the man who feeds on this bread shall live forever."

A reading from the holy gospel according to John

When they pierced his side with a spear,
blood and water flowed out.

Since it was the Preparation Day the Jews did not want to have the bodies left on the cross during the sabbath, for the sabbath was a solemn feast day. They asked Pilate that the legs be broken and the bodies be taken away. Accordingly, the soldiers came and broke the legs of the men crucified with Jesus, first of the one, then of the other. When they came to Jesus and saw that he was already dead, they did not break his legs. One of the soldiers thrust a lance into his side, and immediately blood and water flowed out. (This testimony has been given by an eyewitness, and his testimony is true. He tells what he knows is true, so that you may believe.) These events took place for the fulfillment of Scripture:

"Break none of his bones."

There is still another Scripture passage which says:

"They shall look on him whom they have pierced."

A reading from the holy gospel according to John

Jesus gave the food to his apostles.

At the Sea of Tiberias, Jesus showed himself to the disciples [once again]. This is how the appearance took place. Assembled were Simon Peter, Thomas ("the Twin"), Nathanael (from Cana in Galilee), Zebedee's sons, and two other disciples. Simon Peter said to them, "I am going out to fish." "We will join you," they replied, and went off to get into their boat. All through the night they caught nothing. Just after daybreak Jesus was standing on the shore, though none of the disciples knew it was Jesus. He said to them, "Children, have you caught anything to eat?" "Not a thing," they answered. "Cast your net off to the starboard side," he suggested, "and you will find something." So they made a cast and took so many fish they could not haul the net in. Then the disciple Jesus loved cried out to Peter, "It is the Lord!" On hearing it was the Lord, Simon Peter threw on some clothes—he was stripped—and jumped into the water.

Meanwhile the other disciples came in the boat, towing the net full of fish. Actually they were not far from land—no more than a hundred yards.

When they landed, they saw a charcoal fire there with a fish laid on it and some bread. "Bring some of the fish you just caught," Jesus told them. Simon Peter went aboard and hauled ashore the net loaded with sizable fish—one hundred fifty-three of them! In spite of the great number, the net was not torn.

"Come and eat your meal," Jesus told them. Not one of the disciples presumed to inquire "Who are you?" for they knew it was the Lord. Jesus came over, took the bread and gave it to them, and did the same with the fish. This marked the third time that Jesus appeared to the disciples after being raised from the dead.

READINGS FOR VOTIVE MASSES OF THE SACRED HEART OF JESUS

READINGS FROM THE OLD TESTAMENT

[154.] Exodus 34:4b-7a, 8-9

A reading from the book of Exodus

Our God is merciful and compassionate.

Early in the morning Moses went up Mount Sinai as the Lord had commanded him, taking along the two stone tablets.

Having come down in a cloud, the Lord stood with him there and proclaimed his name, "Lord." Thus the Lord passed before him and cried out, "The Lord, the Lord, a merciful and gracious God, slow to anger and rich in kindness and fidelity." Moses at once bowed down to the ground in worship. Then he said, "If I find favor with you, O Lord, do come along in our company. This is indeed a stiff-necked people; yet pardon our wickedness and sins, and receive us as your own."

[155.] Deuteronomy 7:6-11

A reading from the book of Deuteronomy

God has chosen you because he loves you.

Moses said to the people: "You are a people sacred to the Lord, your God; he has chosen you from all the nations on the face of the earth to be a people peculiarly his own. It was not because you are the largest of all nations that the Lord set his heart on you and chose you, for you are really the smallest of all nations. It was because the Lord loved you and because of his fidelity to the oath he had sworn to your fathers, that he brought you out with his strong hand from the place of slavery, and ransomed you from the hand of Pharoah, king of Egypt. Understand, then, that the Lord, your God, is God indeed, the faithful God who keeps his merciful covenant down to the thousandth generation toward those who love him and keep his commandments, but who repays with destruction the person who hates him; he does not dally with such a one, but makes him personally pay for it. You shall therefore carefully observe the commandments, the statutes and the decrees which I enjoin on you today."

[156.]   Deuteronomy 10:12-22

A reading from the book of Deuteronomy

God loves his chosen ones and their children.

Moses said to the people: "And now, Israel, what does the Lord, your God, ask of you but to fear the Lord, your God, and follow his ways exactly, to love and serve the Lord, your God, with all your heart and all your soul, to keep the commandments and statutes of the Lord which I enjoin on you today for your own good? Think! The heavens, even the highest heavens, belong to the Lord, your God, as well as the earth and everything on it. Yet in his love for your fathers the Lord was so attached to them as to choose you, their descendants, in preference to all other peoples, as indeed he has now done. Circumcise your hearts, therefore, and be no longer stiff-necked. For the Lord, your God, is the God of gods, the Lord of lords, the great God, mighty and awesome, who has no favorites, accepts no bribes; who executes justice for the orphan and the widow, and befriends the alien, feeding and clothing him. So you too must befriend the alien, for you were once aliens yourselves in the land of Egypt. The Lord, your God, shall you fear, and him shall you serve; hold fast to him and swear by his name. He is your glory, he, your God, who has done for you those great and terrible things which your own eyes have seen. Your ancestors went down to Egypt seventy strong, and now the Lord, your God, has made you as numerous as the stars of the sky."

A reading from the book of the prophet Isaiah

Even if a mother forgets her child, I will never forget you.

Sing out, O heavens, and rejoice, O earth,
   break forth into song, you mountains.
For the Lord comforts his people
   and shows mercy to his afflicted.
But Sion said, "The Lord has forsaken me;
   my Lord has forgotten me."
Can a mother forget her infant,
   be without tenderness for the child of her womb?
Even should she forget,
   I will never forget you.

A reading from the book of the prophet Jeremiah

I have loved you with a love that will never end.

At that time, says the Lord,
   I will be the God of all the tribes of Israel,
   and they shall be my people.
      Thus says the Lord:
The people that escaped the sword
   have found favor in the desert.
As Israel comes forward to be given his rest,
   the Lord appears to him from afar:
With age-old love I have loved you;
   so I have kept my mercy toward you.
Again I will restore you, and you shall be rebuilt,
   O virgin Israel;
Carrying your festive tambourines,
   you shall go forth dancing with the merrymakers.

A reading from the book of the prophet Ezekiel

I will take care of my flock.

Thus says the Lord God: I myself will look after and tend my sheep. As a shepherd tends his flock when he finds himself among his scattered sheep, so will I tend my sheep. I will rescue them from every place where they were scattered when it was cloudy and dark. I will lead them out from among the peoples and gather them from the foreign lands; I will bring them back to their own country and pasture them upon the mountains of Israel [in the land's ravines and all its inhabited places]. In good pastures will I pasture them, and on the mountain heights of Israel shall be their grazing ground. There they shall lie down on good grazing ground, and in rich pastures shall they be pastured on the mountains of Israel. I myself will pasture my sheep; I myself will give them rest, says the Lord God. The lost I will seek out, the strayed I will bring back, the injured I will bind up, the sick I will heal [but the sleek and the strong I will destroy], shepherding them rightly.

A reading from the book of the prophet Hosea

My heart is saddened at the thought of parting.

> **The Lord said:**
>
> **When Israel was a child I loved him,**
> **out of Egypt I called my son.**
>
> **Yet it was I who taught Ephraim to walk,**
> **who took them in my arms;**
>
> **I drew them with human cords,**
> **with bands of love;**
>
> **I fostered them like one**
> **who raises an infant to his cheeks;**
>
> **Yet, though I stooped to feed my child,**
> **they did not know that I was their healer.**
>
> **My heart is overwhelmed,**
> **my pity stirred.**
>
> **I will not give vent to my blazing anger,**
> **I will not destroy Ephraim again;**
>
> **For I am God and not man,**
> **the Holy One present among you;**
> **I will not let the flames consume you.**

READINGS FROM THE NEW TESTAMENT

[161.]   Romans 5:5-11

A reading from the letter of Paul to the Romans

Having been justified by his blood, he will be
saved from God's anger through him.

Hope will not leave us disappointed, because the love of God
has been poured out in our hearts through the Holy Spirit who
has been given to us. At the appointed time, when we were still
powerless, Christ died for us godless men. It is rare that anyone
should lay down his life for a just man, though it is barely possible that for a good man someone may have the courage to die.
It is precisely in this that God proves his love for us: that while
we were still sinners, Christ died for us. Now that we have been
justified by his blood, it is all the more certain that we shall be
saved by him from God's wrath. For if, when we were God's
enemies, we were reconciled to him by the death of his Son, it is
all the more certain that we who have been reconciled will be
saved by his life. Not only that; we go so far as to make God our
boast through our Lord Jesus Christ, through whom we have
now received reconciliation.

A reading from the letter of Paul to the Ephesians

He has lavished his rich graces upon us.

Praised be the God and Father of our Lord Jesus Christ, who
has bestowed on us in Christ every spiritual blessing in the
heavens! God chose us in him before the world began, to be holy
and blameless in his sight, to be full of love; likewise he predes-
tined us through Christ Jesus to be his adopted sons—such was
his will and pleasure—that all might praise the divine favor he
has bestowed on us in his beloved.

It is in Christ and through his blood that we have been redeemed and our sins forgiven, so immeasurably generous is
God's favor to us. God has given us the wisdom to understand
fully the mystery, the plan he was pleased to decree in Christ, to
be carried out in the fullness of time: namely, to bring all things
in the heavens and on earth into one under Christ's headship.

A reading from the letter of Paul to the Ephesians

*God has given me the privilege of proclaiming
the riches of Christ to all the nations.*

To me, the least of all believers, was given the grace to preach
to the Gentiles the unfathomable riches of Christ and to en-
lighten all men on the mysterious design which for ages was hidden in God, the Creator of all. Now, therefore, through the
church, God's manifold wisdom is made known to the principal-
ities and powers of heaven, in accord with his age-old purpose,
carried out in Christ Jesus our Lord. In Christ and through faith
in him we can speak freely to God, drawing near him with confi-
dence. Hence, I beg you not to be disheartened by the trials I endure for you; they are your glory.

A reading from the letter of Paul to the Ephesians

I pray that you will grasp the unbounded
love of Christ.

I kneel before the Father from whom every family in heaven and on earth takes its name; and I pray that he will bestow on you gifts in keeping with the riches of his glory. May he strengthen you inwardly through the working of his Spirit. May Christ dwell in your hearts through faith, and may charity be the root and foundation of your life. Thus you will be able to grasp fully, with all the holy ones, the breadth and length and height and depth of Christ's love, and experience this love which surpasses all knowledge, so that you may attain to the fullness of God himself.

A reading from the letter of Paul to the Philippians

May your life be filled with the perfection which comes
through Jesus Christ.

God himself can testify how much I long for each of you with the affection of Christ Jesus! My prayer is that your love may more and more abound, both in understanding and wealth of experience, so that with a clear conscience and blameless conduct you may learn to value the things that really matter, up to the very day of Christ. It is my wish that you may be found rich in the harvest of justice which Jesus Christ has ripened in you, to the glory and praise of God.

A reading from the first letter of John

We love God because he has loved us first.

Beloved,
let us love one another
because love is of God;
everyone who loves is begotten of God
and has knowledge of God.

The man without love has known nothing
   of God,
for God is love.
God's love was revealed in our midst in this
   way:
he sent his only Son to the world
that we might have life through him.
Love, then, consists in this:
not that we have loved God,
but that he has loved us
and has sent his Son as an offering for our
   sins.

Beloved,
if God has loved us so,
we must have the same love for one another.
No one has ever seen God.
Yet if we love one another
God dwells in us,
and his love is brought to perfection in us.
The way we know we remain in him
and he in us
is that he has given us of his Spirit.
We have seen for ourselves, and can testify,

that the Father has sent the Son as Savior
  of the world.
When anyone acknowledges that Jesus is
  the Son of God,
God dwells in him
and he in God.
We have come to know and to believe
in the love God has for us.
God is love,
and he who abides in love
abides in God
and God in him.

[167.]   Revelation 3:14b, 20-22

A reading from the book of Revelation

I will come to eat with you.

The Amen, the faithful Witness and true, the Source of God's creation, has this to say: "Here I stand, knocking at the door. If anyone hears me calling and opens the door, I will enter his house and have supper with him, and he with me. I will give the victor the right to sit with me on my throne, as I myself won the victory and took my seat beside my Father on his throne.

"Let him who has ears heed the Spirit's word to the churches."

A reading from the book of Revelation

You brought us back to God by shedding
your blood for us.

Between the throne with the four living creatures and the
elders, I, John, saw a Lamb standing, a Lamb that had been
slain. He had seven horns and seven eyes; these eyes are the
seven spirits of God, sent to all parts of the world. The Lamb
came and received the scroll from the right hand of the One who
sat on the throne. When he had taken the scroll, the four living
creatures and the twenty-four elders fell down before the
Lamb. Along with their harps the elders were holding vessels of
gold filled with aromatic spices, which were the prayers of
God's holy people. This is the new hymn they sang:

> "Worthy are you to receive the scroll
>   and break open its seals,
>   for you were slain.
> With your blood you purchased for God
>   men of every race and tongue,
>   of every people and nation.
> You made of them a kingdom,
>   and priests to serve our God,
>   and they shall reign on the earth."

As my vision continued, I heard the voices of many angels
who surrounded the throne and the living creatures and the
elders. They were countless in number, thousands and tens of
thousands, and they all cried out:

> "Worthy is the Lamb that was slain
>   to receive power and riches, wisdom and strength,
>   honor and glory and praise!"

RESPONSORIAL PSALM

[169.]   Isaiah 12:2-3, 4, 5-6

℟. (3) You will draw water joyfully
from the springs of salvation.

God indeed is my savior;
I am confident and unafraid.
My strength and my courage is the Lord,
and he has been my savior.
With joy you will draw water
at the fountain of salvation.

℟. You will draw water joyfully
from the springs of salvation.

Give thanks to the Lord, acclaim his name;
among the nations make known his deeds,
proclaim how exalted is his name.

℟. You will draw water joyfully
from the springs of salvation.

Sing praise to the Lord for his glorious
achievement;
let this be known throughout all the earth.
Shout with exultation, O city of Zion,
for great in your midst
is the Holy One of Israel!

℟. You will draw water joyfully
from the springs of salvation.

℟.   (1)   The Lord is my shepherd;
            there is nothing I shall want.

The Lord is my shepherd; I shall not want.
   In verdant pastures he gives me repose;
Beside restful waters he leads me;
   he refreshes my soul.

℟.   The Lord is my shepherd;
            there is nothing I shall want.

Only goodness and kindness follow me
   all the days of my life;
And I shall dwell in the house of the Lord
   for years to come.

℟.   The Lord is my shepherd;
            there is nothing I shall want.

℟.   (6)   Remember your mercies, O Lord.

Your ways, O Lord, make known to me;
   teach me your paths,
Guide me in your truth and teach me,
   for you are God my savior.

℟.   Remember your mercies, O Lord.

Remember that your compassion, O Lord,
and your kindness are from of old.
In your kindness remember me
because of your goodness, O Lord.

℟.　　Remember your mercies, O Lord.

Good and upright is the Lord;
thus he shows sinners the way.
He guides the humble to justice,
he teaches the humble his way.

℟.　　Remember your mercies, O Lord.

All the paths of the Lord are kindness and
constancy
toward those who keep his covenant and his
decrees.
The friendship of the Lord is with those who
fear him,
and his covenant, for their instruction.

℟.　　Remember your mercies, O Lord.

[172.]　　　　　　Psalm 33:1-2, 4-5, 11-12, 18-19, 20-21

℟.　(5)　The earth is full of the goodness of the Lord.

Exult, you just, in the Lord;
praise from the upright is fitting.
Give thanks to the Lord on the harp;
with the ten-stringed lyre chant his praises.

℟.　　The earth is full of the goodness of the Lord.

For upright is the word of the Lord,
   and all his works are trustworthy.
He loves justice and right;
   of the kindness of the Lord the earth is full.

℟. The earth is full of the goodness of the Lord.

But the plan of the Lord stands forever;
   the design of his heart, through all
      generations.
Happy the nation whose God is the Lord,
   the people he has chosen for his own
      inheritance.

℟. The earth is full of the goodness of the Lord.

But see, the eyes of the Lord are upon those
      who fear him,
   upon those who hope for his kindness,
To deliver them from death
   and preserve them in spite of famine.

℟. The earth is full of the goodness of the Lord.

Our soul waits for the Lord,
   who is our help and our shield,
For in him our hearts rejoice;
   in his holy name we trust.

℟. The earth is full of the goodness of the Lord.

℟. (9)   Taste and see the goodness of the Lord.

I will bless the Lord at all times;
   his praise shall be ever in my mouth.
Let my soul glory in the Lord;
   the lowly will hear me and be glad.

℟.   Taste and see the goodness of the Lord.

Glorify the Lord with me,
   let us together extol his name.
I sought the Lord, and he answered me
   and delivered me from all my fears.

℟.   Taste and see the goodness of the Lord.

Look to him that you may be radiant with joy,
   and your faces may not blush with shame.
when the afflicted man called out, the
    Lord heard,
   and from all his distress he saved him.

℟.   Taste and see the goodness of the Lord.

The angel of the Lord encamps
   around those who fear him, and
    delivers them.
Taste and see how good the Lord is;
   happy the man who takes refuge in him.

℟.   Taste and see the goodness of the Lord.

The Lord confronts the evildoers,
to destroy remembrance of them from
the earth.
When the just cry out, the Lord hears them,
and from all their distress he rescues them.

℟.   Taste and see the goodness of the Lord.

The Lord is close to the brokenhearted;
and those who are crushed in spirit he saves.
The Lord redeems the lives of his servants;
no one incurs guilt who takes refuge in him.

℟.   Taste and see the goodness of the Lord.

[174.]   Psalm 103:1-2, 3-4, 6-7, 8, 10

℟.   The Lord's kindness is everlasting
       to those who fear him.

Bless the Lord, O my soul;
and all my being, bless his holy name.
Bless the Lord, O my soul,
and forget not all his benefits.

℟.   The Lord's kindness is everlasting
       to those who fear him.

He pardons all your iniquities,
he heals all your ills.
He redeems your life from destruction,
he crowns you with kindness and compassion.

℟.   The Lord's kindness is everlasting
       to those who fear him.

The Lord secures justice
and the right of all the oppressed.
He has made known his ways to Moses,
and his deeds to the children of Israel.

℟. The Lord's kindness is everlasting
to those who fear him.

Merciful and gracious is the Lord,
slow to anger and abounding in kindness.
Not according to our sins does he deal with us,
nor does he requite us according to our
crimes.

℟. The Lord's kindness is everlasting
to those who fear him.

ALLELUIA VERSE
AND VERSE BEFORE THE GOSPEL

[175.]   Matthew 11:25

Blessed are you, Father, Lord of heaven and
    earth;
You have revealed to little ones the mysteries
    of the kingdom.

[176.]   Matthew 11:28

Come to me, all you that labor and are
    burdened,
and I will give you rest, says the Lord.

[177.]   Matthew 11:29

Take my yoke upon you;
learn from me, for I am gentle and lowly in
    heart.

[178.]   John 10:14

I am the good shepherd, says the Lord;
I know my sheep, and mine know me.

[179.]   John 15:9

As the Father has loved me, so have I loved
    you;
remain in my love.

[180.]   1 John 4:10

God first loved us
and sent his Son to take away our sins.

GOSPEL

[181.]   Matthew 11:25-30

A reading from the holy gospel according to Matthew

I am meek and humble of heart.

Jesus said: "Father, Lord of heaven and earth, to you I offer praise; for what you have hidden from the learned and the clever you have revealed to the merest children. Father, it is true. You have graciously willed it so. Everything has been given over to me by my Father. No one knows the Son but the Father, and no one knows the Father but the Son—and anyone to whom the Son wishes to reveal him.

"Come to me, all you who are weary and find life burdensome, and I will refresh you. Take my yoke upon your shoulders and learn from me, for I am gentle and humble of heart. Your souls will find rest, for my yoke is easy and my burden light."

[182.]   Luke 15:1-10

A reading from the holy gospel according to Luke

Heaven is filled with joy when one sinner
turns back to God.

The tax collectors and sinners were all gathering around Jesus to hear him, at which the Pharisees murmured, "This man welcomes sinners and eats with them." Then he addressed this parable to them: "Who among you, if he has a hundred sheep and loses one of them, does not leave the ninety-nine in the wasteland and follow the lost one until he finds it? And when he finds it, he puts it on his shoulders in jubilation. Once arrived home, he invites friends and neighbors in and says to them, 'Rejoice with me because I have found my lost sheep.' I tell you, there will likewise be more joy in heaven over one repentant sinner than over ninety-nine righteous people who have no need to repent.

"What woman, if she has ten silver pieces and loses one, does not light a lamp and sweep the house in a diligent search until she has retrieved what she has lost? And when she finds it, she calls in her friends and neighbors to say, 'Rejoice with me! I have found the silver piece I lost.' I tell you, there will be the same kind of joy before the angels of God over one repentant sinner."

[183.]   Luke 15:1-3, 11-32

A reading from the holy gospel according to Luke

We are celebrating because your brother has
come back from death.

The tax collectors and sinners were all gathering around Jesus to hear him, at which the Pharisees murmured, "This man welcomes sinners and eats with them." Then he addressed this parable to them:

"A man had two sons. The younger of them said to his father, 'Father, give me the share of the estate that is coming to me.' So the father divided up the property. Some days later this younger son collected all his belongings and went off to a distant land, where he squandered his money on dissolute living. After he had spent everything, a great famine broke out in that country and he was in dire need. So he attached himself to one of the propertied class of the place, who sent him to his farm to take care of the pigs. He longed to fill his belly with the husks that were fodder for the pigs, but no one made a move to give him anything. Coming to his senses at last, he said: 'How many hired hands at my father's place have more than enough to eat, while here I am starving! I will break away and return to my father, and say to him, "Father, I have sinned against God and against you; I no longer deserve to be called your son. Treat me like one of your hired hands".' With that he set off for his father's house. While he was still a long way off, his father caught sight of him and was deeply moved. He ran out to meet him, threw his arms around his neck, and kissed him. The son said to him, 'Father, I have sinned against God and against you; I no longer deserve to be called your son.' The father said to his servants: 'Quick! bring out the finest robe and put it on him; put a ring on his finger and shoes on his feet. Take the fatted calf and kill it. Let us eat and celebrate because this son of mine was dead and has come back to life. He was lost and is found.' Then the celebration began.

"Meanwhile the elder son was out on the land. As he neared the house on his way home, he heard the sound of music and dancing. He called one of the servants and asked him the reason for the dancing and the music. The servant answered, 'Your brother is home, and your father has killed the fatted calf because he has him back in good health.' The son grew angry at this and would not go in; but his father came out and began to plead with him.

"He said to his father: in reply, 'For years now I have slaved for you. I never disobeyed one of your orders, yet you never gave me so much as a kid goat to celebrate with my friends. Then, when this son of yours returns after having gone through your property with loose women, you kill the fatted calf for him.'

" 'My son,' replied the father, 'you are with me always, and everything I have is yours. But we had to celebrate and rejoice! This brother of yours was dead, and has come back to life. He was lost, and is found'."

A reading from the holy gospel according to John

A good shepherd is ready to die for his flock.

Jesus said to his disciples:

"I am the good shepherd;
the good shepherd lays down his life for
    the sheep.
The hired hand who is no shepherd,
nor owner of the sheep,
catches sight of the wolf coming
and runs away, leaving the sheep
to be snatched and scattered by the wolf.
This is because he works for pay;
he has no concern for the sheep.
"I am the good shepherd.
I know my sheep
and my sheep know me
in the same way that the Father knows me
and I know the Father;
for these sheep I will give my life.
I have other sheep
that do not belong to this fold.
I must lead them, too,
and they shall hear my voice.
There shall be one flock then, one shepherd.
The Father loves me for this:
that I lay down my life
to take it up again.
No one takes it from me;
I lay it down freely.
I have power to lay it down,
and I have power to take it up again.
This command I received from my Father."

A reading from the holy gospel according to John

Live in me as I live in you.

Jesus said to his disciples:

"I am the true vine
and my Father is the vinegrower.
He prunes away
every barren branch,
but the fruitful ones
he trims clean
to increase their yield.
You are clean already,
thanks to the word I have spoken to you.
Live on in me, as I do in you.
No more than a branch can bear fruit of
    itself
apart from the vine,
can you bear fruit
apart from me.
I am the vine, you are the branches.
He who lives in me and I in him,
will produce abundantly,
for apart from me you can do nothing.
A man who does not live in me
is like a withered, rejected branch,
picked up to be thrown in the fire and burnt.
If you live in me,
and my words stay part of you,
you may ask what you will—
it will be done for you.
My Father has been glorified
in your bearing much fruit
and becoming my disciples."

A reading from the holy gospel according to John

Love one another as much as I love you.

Jesus said to his disciples:

"As the Father has loved me,
so I have loved you.
Live on in my love.
You will live in my love
if you keep my commandments,
even as I have kept my Father's commandments,
and live in his love.
All this I tell you
that my joy may be yours
and your joy may be complete.
This is my commandment:
love one another
as I have loved you.
There is no greater love than this:
to lay down one's life for one's friends.
You are my friends
if you do what I command you.
I no longer speak of you as slaves,
for a slave does not know what his master
  is about.
Instead, I call you friends,
since I have made known to you all that I
  heard from my Father.
It was not you who chose me,
it was I who chose you
to go forth and bear fruit.
Your fruit must endure,
so that all you ask the Father in my name
he will give you.
The command I give you is this,
that you love one another."

A reading from the holy gospel according to John

Father, you loved them as you loved me.

Jesus looked up to heaven and prayed:

"Holy Father,
I do not pray for my disciples alone.
I pray also for those who will believe in me
through their word,
that all may be one
as you, Father, are in me, and I in you;
I pray that they may be [one] in us,
that the world may believe that you sent me.
I have given them the glory you gave me
that they may be one, as we are one—
I living in them, you living in me—
that their unity may be complete.
So shall the world know that you sent me,
and that you loved them as you loved me.
Father,
all those you gave me
I would have in my company
where I am,
to see this glory of mine
which is your gift to me,
because of the love you bore me before the
    world began.
Just Father,
the world has not known you,
but I have known you;
and these men have known that you sent me.
To them I have revealed your name,
and I will continue to reveal it
so that your love for me may live in them,
and I may live in them."

A reading from the holy gospel according to John

When they pierced his side with a spear, blood
and water flowed out.

Since it was the Preparation Day the Jews did not want to
have the bodies left on the cross during the sabbath, for that
sabbath was a solemn feast day. They asked Pilate that the legs
be broken and the bodies be taken away. Accordingly, the soldiers came and broke the legs of the men crucified with Jesus,
first of the one, then of the other. When they came to Jesus and
saw that he was already dead, they did not break his legs. One of
the soldiers thrust a lance into his side, and immediately blood
and water flowed out. (This testimony has been given by an eyewitness, and his testimony is true. He tells what he knows is
true, so that you may believe.) These events took place for the
fulfillment of Scripture:

"Break none of his bones."

There is still another Scripture passage which says:

"They shall look on him whom they have
    pierced."

APPENDIX II

SOLEMN BLESSINGS

1.

May the Lord bless you and keep you.   ℟. Amen.

May his face shine upon you,
and be gracious to you.   ℟. Amen.

May he look upon you with kindness,
and give you his peace.   ℟. Amen.

May almighty God bless you,
the Father, and the Son, ✛ and the Holy Spirit.   ℟. Amen.

2.

May the peace of God
which is beyond all understanding
keep your hearts and minds
in the knowledge and love of God
and of his Son, our Lord Jesus Christ.   ℟. Amen.

May almighty God bless you,
the Father, and the Son, ✛ and the Holy Spirit.   ℟. Amen.

3.

May almighty God bless you in his mercy,
and make you always aware of his saving wisdom.   ℟. Amen.

May he strengthen your faith with proofs of his love,
so that you will persevere in good works.   ℟. Amen.

May he direct your steps to himself,
and show you how to walk in charity and peace.　℟. Amen.

May almighty God bless you,
the Father, and the Son, ✚ and the Holy Spirit.　℟. Amen.

4.

May the God of all consolation
bless you in every way
and grant you peace all the days of your life.　℟. Amen.

May he free you from all anxiety
and strengthen your hearts in his love.　℟. Amen.

May he enrich you with his gifts of faith, hope, and love,
so that what you do in this life
will bring you to the happiness of everlasting life.　℟. Amen.

May almighty God bless you,
the Father, and the Son, ✚ and the Holy Spirit.　℟. Amen.

5.

May almighty God keep you from all harm
and bless you with every good gift.　℟. Amen.

May he set his Word in your heart
and fill you with lasting joy.　℟. Amen.

May you walk in his ways,
always knowing what is right and good,
until you enter your heavenly inheritance.　℟. Amen.

May almighty God bless you,
the Father, and the Son, ✚ and the Holy Spirit.　℟. Amen.